This journal belongs to:

_____

Tips for manifesting your every desire

- Visualize your dream life

- Recite daily affirmations

- Get rid of negative limiting beliefs

- Train your mind to only focus on the good

- Choose your thoughts wisely

- Speak positively over your life

- Align your actions with your goals

- Give up the need to control everything

- Trust the process

I am the architect of my life; I build its foundation and choose its contents.

Manifestation Planner

Month: _____

Things I'm manifesting this month:

Thing:	Deadline:
☆	
☆	
☆	
☆	
☆	

Positive affirmations:

_____
_____
_____
_____
_____
_____

Notes & Reminders:

_____
_____
_____
_____

Notes

I am superior to negative thoughts and low actions.

Manifestation Planner

Month: _____

Things I'm manifesting this month:

Thing:	Deadline:
☆	
☆	
☆	
☆	
☆	

Positive affirmations:

_____
_____
_____
_____
_____
_____

Notes & Reminders:

_____
_____
_____
_____

Notes

I have been given endless talents which I begin to utilize today.

Manifestation Planner

Month: _____

Things I'm manifesting this month:

Thing:	Deadline:
☆	
☆	
☆	
☆	
☆	

Positive affirmations:

_____
_____
_____
_____
_____
_____

Notes & Reminders:

_____
_____
_____
_____

Notes

Manifestation Planner

Month: _____

Things I'm manifesting this month:

Thing:	Deadline:
☆	
☆	
☆	
☆	
☆	

Positive affirmations:

_____
_____
_____
_____
_____
_____

Notes & Reminders:

_____
_____
_____
_____

Notes

I am brimming with energy and overflowing with joy.

Manifestation Planner

Month: _____

Things I'm manifesting this month:

Thing:	Deadline:
☆	
☆	
☆	
☆	
☆	

Positive affirmations:

_____
_____
_____
_____
_____
_____

Notes & Reminders:

_____
_____
_____
_____

Notes

Happiness is a choice. I base my happiness on my own accomplishments and the blessings I've been given.

Manifestation Planner

Month: _____

Things I'm manifesting this month:

Thing:	Deadline:
☆	
☆	
☆	
☆	
☆	

Positive affirmations:

_____
_____
_____
_____
_____
_____

Notes & Reminders:

_____
_____
_____
_____

Notes

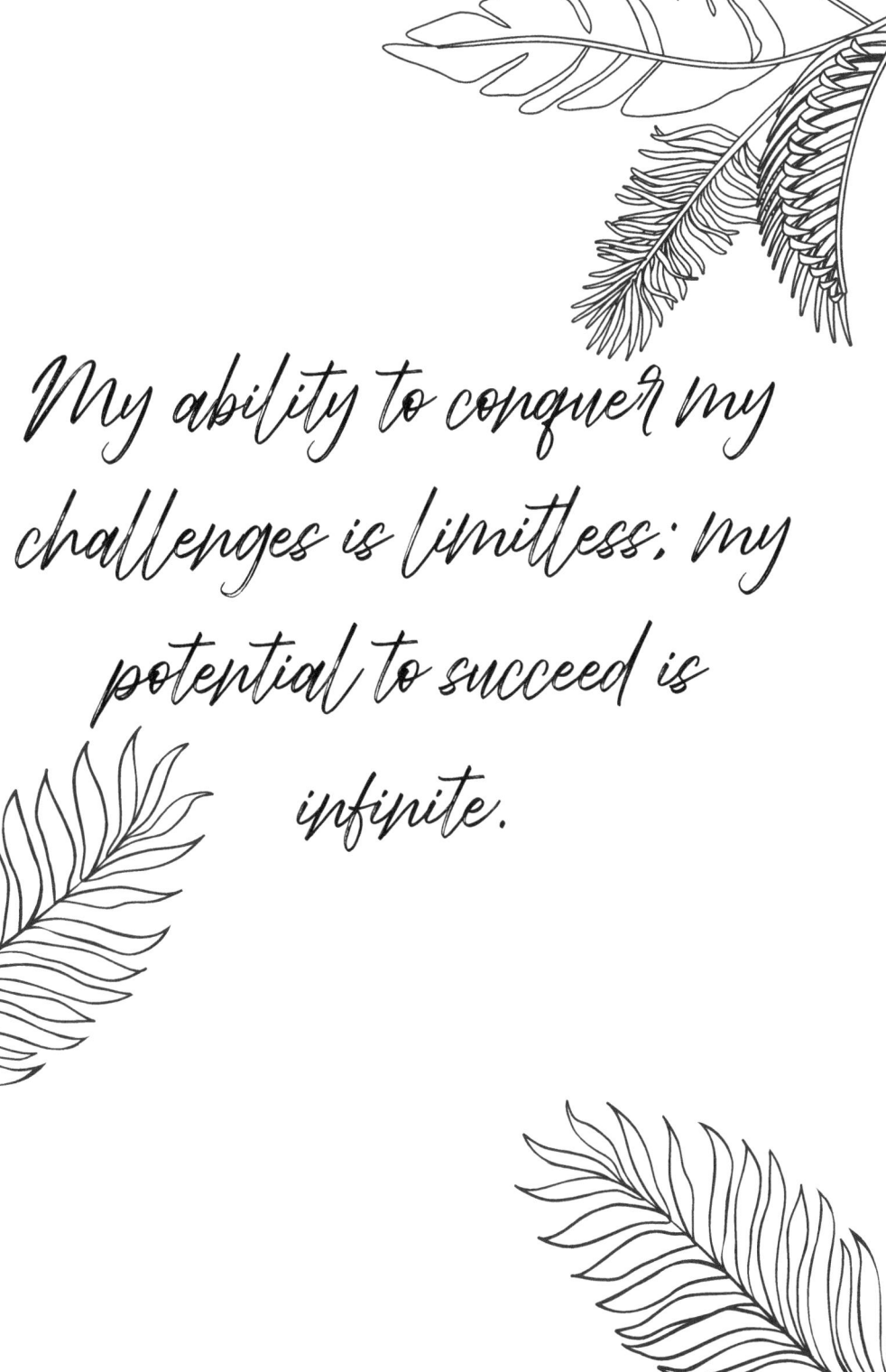

My ability to conquer my challenges is limitless; my potential to succeed is infinite.

Manifestation Planner

Month: _____

Things I'm manifesting this month:

Thing:	Deadline:
☆	
☆	
☆	
☆	
☆	

Positive affirmations:

_____
_____
_____
_____
_____
_____

Notes & Reminders:

_____
_____
_____
_____

Notes

I am courageous and I stand up for myself.

Manifestation Planner

Month: _____

Things I'm manifesting this month:

Thing:	Deadline:
☆	
☆	
☆	
☆	
☆	

Positive affirmations:

_____
_____
_____
_____
_____
_____

Notes & Reminders:

_____
_____
_____
_____

Notes

Today, I abandon my old habits and take up new, more positive ones.

Manifestation Planner

Month: _____

Things I'm manifesting this month:

Thing:	Deadline:
☆	
☆	
☆	
☆	
☆	

Positive affirmations:

_____
_____
_____
_____
_____
_____

Notes & Reminders:

_____
_____
_____
_____

Notes

I am blessed with an incredible family and wonderful friends.

Manifestation Planner

Month: _____

Things I'm manifesting this month:

Thing:	Deadline:
☆	
☆	
☆	
☆	
☆	

Positive affirmations:

_____
_____
_____
_____
_____
_____

Notes & Reminders:

_____
_____
_____
_____

Notes

Many people look up to me and recognize my worth; I am admired.

Manifestation Planner

Month: _____

Things I'm manifesting this month:

Thing:	Deadline:
☆	
☆	
☆	
☆	
☆	

Positive affirmations:

_____
_____
_____
_____
_____
_____

Notes & Reminders:

_____
_____
_____
_____

Notes

I acknowledge my own self-worth; my confidence is soaring.

Manifestation Planner

Month: _____

Things I'm manifesting this month:

Thing:	Deadline:
☆	
☆	
☆	
☆	
☆	

Positive affirmations:
_____
_____
_____
_____
_____
_____

Notes & Reminders:
_____
_____
_____
_____

Notes

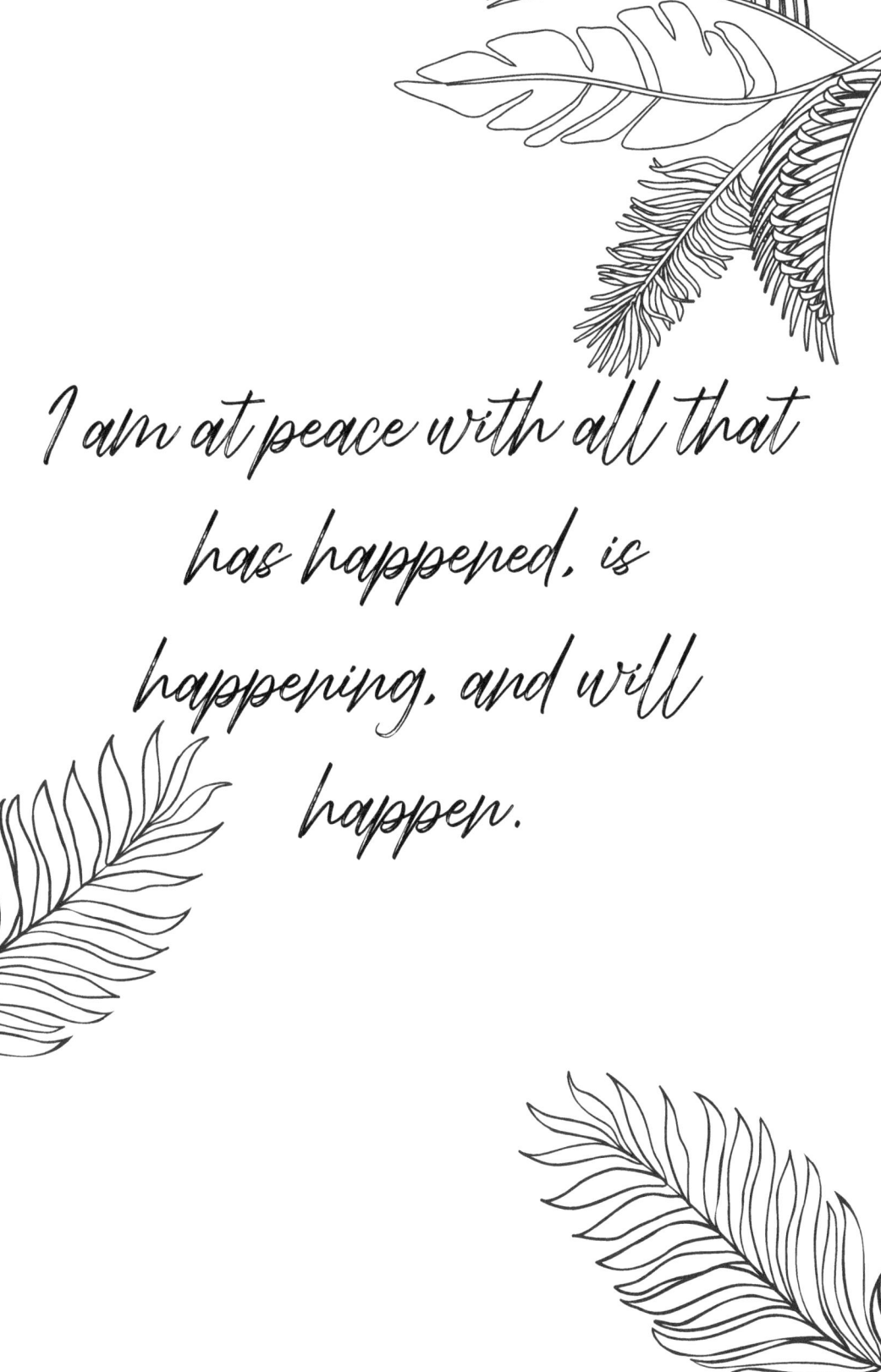

I am at peace with all that has happened, is happening, and will happen.

Manifest that shit!

Manifest that shit!

Manifest that shit!

Manifest that shit!

Manifest that shit!

Manifest that shit!

Manifest that shit!

Manifest that shit!

Manifest that shit!

Manifest that shit!

Manifest that shit!

Manifest that shit!

Manifest that shit!

Manifest that shit!

Manifest that shit!

Manifest that shit!

Manifest that shit!

Manifest that shit!

Manifest that shit!

Manifest that shit!

Manifest that shit!

Manifest that shit!

Manifest that shit!

Manifest that shit!

Manifest that shit!

Manifest that shit!

Manifest that shit!

Manifest that shit!

Manifest that shit!

Manifest that shit!

Manifest that shit!

Manifest that shit!

Manifest that shit!

Manifest that shit!

Manifest that shit!

Manifest that shit!

Manifest that shit!

Manifest that shit!

Manifest that shit!

Manifest that shit!

Manifest that shit!

Manifest that shit!

Manifest that shit!

Manifest that shit!

Manifest that shit!

Manifest that shit!

Manifest that shit!

Manifest that shit!

Manifest that shit!

Manifest that shit!

Manifest that shit!

Manifest that shit!

Manifest that shit!

Manifest that shit!

Manifest that shit!

Manifest that shit!

Manifest that shit!

Manifest that shit!

Manifest that shit!

Manifest that shit!

Manifest that shit!

www.ingramcontent.com/pod-product-compliance
Ingram Content Group UK Ltd.
Pitfield, Milton Keynes, MK11 3LW, UK
UKHW022223230426
12048UKWH00016BA/1020